SINAI

EGYPT POCKET GUIDE

Alberto Siliotti

THE AMERICAN UNIVERSITY IN CAIRO PRESS

Text and Photographs Alberto Siliotti
Drawings Stefania Cossu
English Translation Richard Pierce

General Editing Yvonne Marzoni
Graphic Design Geodia

Copyright © 2000 by Geodia (Verona, Italy)

This edition first published in Egypt jointly by
The American University in Cairo Press (Cairo and New York)
Elias Modern Publishing House (Cairo)
Geodia (Verona, Italy)

Created by Geodia (Verona, Italy)
Printed in Egypt by Elias Modern Publishing House (Cairo)
Distributed by the American University in Cairo Press (Cairo and New York)

ISBN 977 424 597 0

Dar el Kutub No. 9215/00

Contents

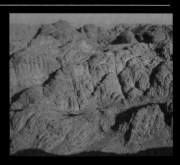

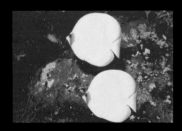

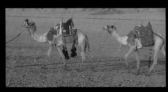

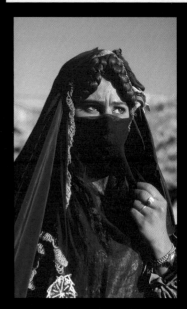

Sinai

*S*inai is a triangular-shaped
peninsula situated between the
continents of Asia and Africa; geologically it is
part of the latter.

The Sinai peninsula is
about 380 kilometers
long and 210 km wide
and has a surface area of
about 61,000 square
kilometers. It juts into the
Red Sea, separating the
northern part into two
deep arms—the Gulf of
Suez to the west and the
Gulf of Aqaba to the east.
The low and sandy
northern coast of Sinai is
washed by the
Mediterranean Sea, while
its mountainous central-
southern section ends in
two peaks a short
distance from each other:
Gebel Musa (Moses'
Mountain, or Mount Sinai,

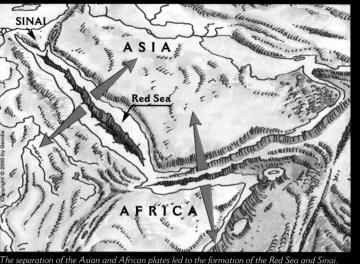

The separation of the Asian and African plates led to the formation of the Red Sea and Sinai.

2,285 m); and *Gebel Katrin*, which is the highest point in the Sinai peninsula and in Egypt (2,637 m).

Sinai is mentioned in the Bible (*Exodus 16, 1; Exodus 19, 1; Numbers 10, 11*), but the origin of the name is still unclear. Some scholars believe it may have derived from *Sin*, the name of an ancient moon god.

Mount Sinai

Profile from the Gulf of Suez to the Gulf of Aqaba, with Gebel Katrin and the Sinai peninsula between them.

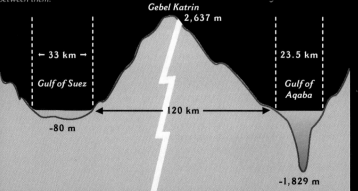

The Geology and Climate

*T*he central-southern part of Sinai is a mountainous desert with an average altitude of about 1,500 meters a.s.l.; its geological nucleus consists of Precambrian crystalline magmatic rocks.

The effects of erosion on sandstone

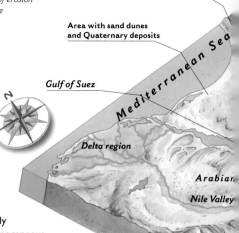

Tertiary era limestones and sandstones in the Tih Plateau

Jurassic limestones at Gebel Maghara

Area with sand dunes and Quaternary deposits

Gulf of Suez

Mediterranean Sea

Delta region

Arabian

Nile Valley

Libyan

*T*here are three extremely different areas in Sinai. The first, in the north, consists of sand dunes and Quatenary deposits along the age-old *wadis* (fossilized stream beds that are usually dry but may at times become active in the rainy season) and by fossil beaches created by the change in the level of the Mediterranean during the alternating glacial and interglacial periods that characterized the Quaternary era, which began about two million years ago. This area is fairly homogeneous, consisting of a rather flat and uniform terrain that is interrupted to the south by a series of Cretaceous limestone outcrops and the impressive Gebel Maghara massif, made up of Jurassic limestone and sandstone. South of the *Gebel Maghara* range, in the middle of the Sinai peninsula, is the beginning of the second area, in which Quaternary formations are interrupted by numerous wide Tertiary limestone outcrops (dating from the Eocene and, more rarely, the

Sandstone colored by iron oxides

Alluvium deposits

Granite with veins of basalt

Precambrian granites with veins of basalt in the St. Catherine region

Gulf of Aqaba

Quaternary fossil coral formations

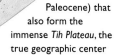

R e d   S e a

Desert

Desert

Watercourse

of the Sinai peninsula. This plateau extends southward and is bordered by Cretaceous limestone outcrops that separate it from a zone of Precambrian magmatic rocks which for the most part consist of granitic rock (granite, granodiorite, and gabbro) and basalt, which can be identified easily by their blackish color. The basalt is the result of volcanic activity on the ocean bottom. The volcanic zone is bordered, especially to the west, by stretches of Quarternary outcrops, ancient coral formations that also constitute the southern tip of the peninsula.

Climate

Sinai enjoys a typical desert climate: hot and dry, with significant differences in temperature between day and night that are more marked due to the presence of mountains over 2,000 meters high (in some cases the temperature range may be as much as 30° centigrade). The best times to visit Sinai are autumn (October and November) and spring (March and April), when the sky is clearer, the oasis vegetation is greener and the springs have plenty of water.

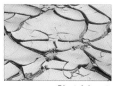

Pluvial deposits

Paleocene) that also form the immense *Tih Plateau*, the true geographic center

Fossil coral

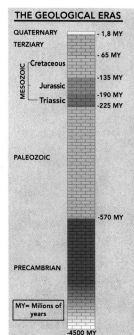

THE GEOLOGICAL ERAS

QUATERNARY		- 1,8 MY
TERZIARY		- 65 MY
MESOZOIC	Cretaceous	-135 MY
	Jurassic	-190 MY
	Triassic	-225 MY
PALEOZOIC		-570 MY
PRECAMBRIAN		
MY= Milions of years		
		-4500 MY

The Fauna

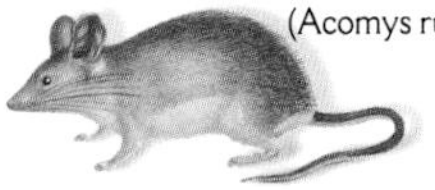
Golden spiny mouse (Acomys russatus)

The land fauna in Sinai includes gazelles, foxes, ibexes, small rodents, and lizards. There is also a large number of birds such as seagulls, falcons, herons, and the migratory species, while the sea fauna numbers over 1,000 species of pelagic and coral fish, mollusks, and 170 species of coral.

*Red fox (*Vulpes vulpes*) in the Ras Mohammed National Park*

Despite the arid climate the Sinai peninsula has a good number of land fauna, consisting mostly of foxes, ruminants, and some genera of reptiles. The red fox (*Vulpes vulpes*) and the rarer sand fox (*Vulpes rueppelli*) are often seen at the edges of the desert near inhabited areas, where they roam about in search of food and water. The ruminants are less abundant. The most typical species are the ibex (*Capra ibex nubiana*), a sort of local chamois that has splendid arched horns that may be over 70 centimeters long, and the dorcas gazelle (*Gazella dorcas*). The ibex, once a common inhabitant of the impracticable craggy Sinai environment, had almost become extinct because of indiscriminate hunting practices in the early 20th century. However, it is now slowly beginning to repopulate the mountains in the Gebel Katrin region. And though

*Osprey (*Pandion haliaetus*)*

Sinai agama

Uromastix ornatus

the gazelles have become rare, they are increasing in number, especially in the flat desert areas suitable for these timid animals that live in herds and need large open spaces as their habitat. The rodents are much more numerous. The

Rock hyrax (*Procavia capensis*)

White-eyed gulls (*Larus leucophthalmus*) **A** and the western reef heron (*Egretta gularis*) **B**

most representative of these animals in Sinai are the golden spiny mouse (*Acomys russatus*) and the rather rare Sinai rock hyrax (*Procavia syriaca capensis*). Among the reptiles are two species of lizards worth mentioning: the small Sinai agama (*Agama sinaitica*), with its characteristic turquoise-blue head and neck,

Egyptian vulture (*Neophron percnopterus*)

carpet viper (*Echis coloratus*), and the timid and harmless Egyptian sand snake (*Psammophis schokari aegyptius*). Sinai boasts an abundance of birds. The most common are the herons, especially the western reef heron (*Egretta gularis*), which lives in colonies and is quite widespread in the mangrove areas, where it finds shelter among the branches; the white-eyed gull (*Larus leucophthalmus*), which is an

indigeneous species; the *Sterna caspia* tern; the large osprey (*Pandion haliaetus*), a typical diurnal raptor that feeds on small fish and is a sedentary inhabitant of the Strait of Tiran; and the white Egyptian vulture (*Neophron percnopterus*),

Tern (*Sterna sp.*)

which really lives in the Red Sea area only in the summer.

Gazella dorcas

and the large and much rarer dabb lizard (*Uromastix ornatus*). In the sandy and rocky desert areas you may come across some snakes, such as the horned viper (*Cerastes cerastes*), the Burton's

Ibex (*Capra ibex nubiana*)

Storks and Migratory Birds

*E*very year around the end of August the skies in Sinai are filled with tens of thousands of storks coming from Europe to stop on their way to South Africa.

White stork

The arrival of the white storks at the Ras Mohammed National Park

*S*inai lies along one of the major bird migration routes. The birds spend the winter in South Africa and then in early spring begin the long journey back to Europe along the same route.

For a couple of weeks in the latter half of August about 500,000 white storks (*Ciconia ciconia*) fly through the skies of Sinai and stop at the edges of the bays at Ras Mohammed or in the tranquil waters of Nabq protected by the mangrove forests.

However, many storks arrive in Sinai not only exhausted but also in very poor physical condition because of the progressive deterioration of their European habitats (where pesticides are commonly used), the growing scarcity of countryside not used for agriculture, and the spread of electrification networks, which means more risk of electrocution for the birds.

Although storks are undoubtedly the most

White stork (Ciconia ciconia)

Golden eagle
(Aquila
chrysaetos)

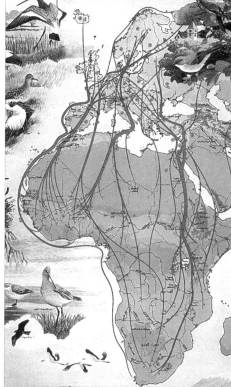

Main routes of migratory birds

important migratory birds in Sinai, there are also other species from the north Mediterranean area and southwestern Asia that come to Egypt to spend the winter in the Nile Valley or in the lagoons of northern Sinai. Some of the birds in this category are eagles—the golden eagle (Aquila chrysaetos), imperial eagle (Aquila heliaca), step eagle Aquila nipalensis, and lesser

Sanderling sandpiper
(Calidris alba)

Quail
(Coturnix
coturnix)

spotted eagle Aquila pomarina; plovers such as Charadrius alexandrinus and Hoplopterus spinosus; the Sanderling sandpiper

(Calidris alba), which is found most of all in the Lake Bardawil region near El-Arish; and the innumerable quails (Coturnix coturnix).

THE WHITE STORK

On an average the white stork (Ciconia ciconia) is from 80 to 100 centimeters tall and weighs 3–4 kilos. This bird prefers to nest in elevated places such the tops of dead trees and house roofs. The female lays 3–5 eggs that hatch after about a month; the young leave their nest when they are two months old.

The Flora

*The most common forest tree in Sinai is the acacia tree (*Acacia raddiana*)*

*I*n Sinai the flora consists mostly of large acacia trees and small shrubs and is extremely interesting because of the variety of its species, which number more than 800, 34 of which are endemic, that is to say, found only in the region.

It might seem strange that plants and shrubs should grow in such a desolate landscape, but their adaptive capacity is truly amazing. In fact, there is practically no wadi without large acacias (*Acacia raddiana* and *Acacia tortilis*, called *seyal* in Arabic), which are among the most typical representatives of forest trees in the Sinai peninsula.

The harsh living conditions in this barren land have triggered a series of transformations in the structural organs

*Green capparis (*Capparis sinaica*)*

of the plants and shrubs that have enabled them to adapt to the environment. Naturally, better conditions for flora are to be found in

the oases, where water is relatively plentiful, favoring the growth of date palms

(*Phoenix dactylifera*) and tamarisks (*Tamarix nilotica* and *T. mannifera*). The latter have been known since Biblical times as the source of manna, the sweet edible secretion.

Sinai also has willow trees (called *safsafa* in Arabic) and fruit trees such as olives (*zeitun* in Arabic), pomegranates (*Punica granatum*, *rumman* in Arabic), and figs (*Ficus pseudosycomorus*). Figs can also be seen growing in the beds of the wadis together with Sodom-apples (*Calotropa procera*), which are poisonous. But the true wealth of plant life in Sinai is the extraordinary variety and abundance of shrubs such as the the green capparis (*Capparis sinaica*) that thrive even on the steep granite cliff faces, and the huge expanses of Artemisia judaica mugwort (*betheran* in Arabic) and *habak* or *Mentha sylvestris* mint. Many of these wild shrubs are also commonly used by the Bedouins to make herbal infusions, as either

A "desert pumpkin"

Sodom-apples

drinks or medicine. For example, *habak* is used to flavor tea, while *handal* or "desert pumpkin" (*Citrullus colocynthis* which belongs to the *Coloquintidae* family) is used in an herbal infusion that is a cathartic.

*A date palm (*Phoenix dactylifera*) in the Ain Khudra Oasis*

THE BURNING BUSH

Certainly the most famous shrub in Sinai is found at St. Catherine's Monastery: the **Rubus sanctus** *bramble, which is common in the Mediterranean and is traditionally thought to be the bush that Moses saw burn without being consumed (*Exodus 3,2*).*

NATURAL ENVIRONMENTS

Coral Reef

Mangroves

Desert

Oases

The Coral Reef

An emperor angelfish
(Pomacanthus imperator)

*T*he coral reef that borders most of
the Sinai coastline is considered one
of the most beautiful in the world. It boasts incredibly
varied and abundant fauna, which has earned the sea
bottom the nickname of "Allah's Garden."

The Ras Nasrani coral reef

Acropores are one of the typical reef madrepores

The coral reefs are the
result of the building
activity of madrepores,
which are commonly
known as corals even
though strictly speaking
this term should be used
for the Mediterranean
red coral, *Corallium
rubrum*. The coral reefs
are particularly well
developed along the
coasts of Sinai and,
generally, of the Red Sea,
where environmental
conditions are ideal for
their growth and proli-
feration: warm, clear,
unpolluted water with a

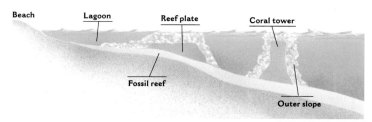

Beach   Lagoon   Reef plate   Coral tower

Fossil reef

Outer slope

Section of a fringing reef

temperature never below 20° centigrade. Coral reefs have an extra-ordinary gamut of animal species that range from microscopic creatures to large ones such as manta rays, sharks, and dolphins. The very structure of the reef offers shelter to many species of animals both during their repro-duction and early stages and during their entire lifetime.

One need only move a few meters away from the reef to note a drastic decrease in the variety and density of the fish. Coral reefs can be classified into three main types according to their topographical features: fringing reefs, barrier reefs, and atolls. Almost all the reefs of Sinai and

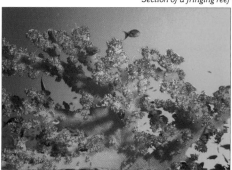

A typical example of Alcyonacea or soft corals (genus Dendronephtya)

the Red Sea are fringing reefs, which grow in parallel fringes close to the coastline, from which they are often separated by a lagoon.

A group of gorgonians

CORAL POLYPS

Coral polyps are the basic element of corals—organisms belonging to the phylum Cnidaria, which also includes jellyfish and sea anemones. The coral polyp consists of a double wall of cells (epiderma and gastroderma) that form mobile tentacles and surround the gastrovascular cavity. Cnidaria have an infinite number of shapes and sizes, both the soft

corals (Alcyonacea) and stony corals (for example, the Acropora, or typical madrepores). The latter secrete a calcareous calyx that protects the polyp from its highly competitive environment.

When eating, coral polyps use their tentacles to take food to their mouth; they feed on plankton, small crayfish, and sometimes even tiny fish.

tentacles

mouth

epiderma   theca

gastroderma   gastrovascular cavity

FIRE CORAL

On the surface of the corals' tentacles there are microscopic bacteria with special stinging cells known as nematocysts; when provoked, these cells quickly turn their cirri outward and sting the 'intruder.' The effect of the sting varies from genus to genus; the so-called fire corals, which belong to the genus Millepora, have the strongest sting.

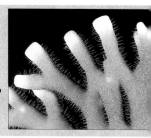

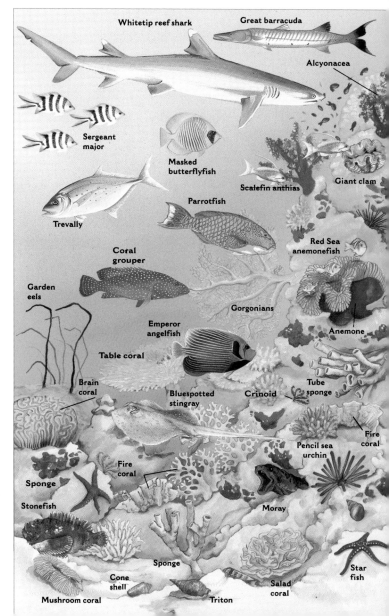

Whitetip reef shark
Great barracuda
Alcyonacea
Sergeant major
Masked butterflyfish
Scalefin anthias
Giant clam
Parrotfish
Trevally
Red Sea anemonefish
Coral grouper
Garden eels
Gorgonians
Anemone
Emperor angelfish
Table coral
Tube sponge
Brain coral
Bluespotted stingray
Crinoid
Fire coral
Sponge
Fire coral
Pencil sea urchin
Stonefish
Moray
Sponge
Star fish
Mushroom coral
Cone shell
Triton
Salad coral

Mangroves

With their capacity to filter sea water by eliminating the salt through their leaves, these tropical evergreen trees are among the most unusual plants in Sinai and an essential part of a delicate ecosystem.

The mangroves at Nabq

The special plants commonly known as mangroves (their scientific name is *Avicenia marina*) thrive in some coastal zones of Sinai. The mangrove trees are concentrated mostly at Ras Mohammed, where they are lined along the

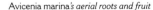

Avicenia marina's aerial roots and fruit

canal that separates an islet—aptly named "Mangrove Island"—from the land, and above all at Nabq, a locality a few kilometers north of the Ras Nasrani airport. The mangroves in Sinai are important from a scientific standpoint in that they are the northernmost specimens in the entire Red Sea–Indian Ocean area. They are singular plants because they feed upon sea water, which they filter by eliminating the

Uca sp.

Macrophthalmus sp.

Scylla sp.

Pirenella calliauda

Pinna bicolor

Mangroves

Seagrass (Halophila stipulacea)

Lagoon

Fossil reef

High tide

Low tide

The complex mangrove ecosystem

salt through their leaves, while oxygen is absorbed directly from the air by means of a highly developed network of sub-aerial roots.

Mangrove forests are an ideal habitat for many sea animals, for several genera of crustaceans (genus *Uca* sp., *Macrophthalmus* sp., *Scylla* sp.) as well as numerous species of birds and some genera of algae, mostly *Halophila stipulacea* and *Caulerpa* sp. Small fish find shelter in the tangled network of mangrove roots, where they also lay their eggs, while birds nest among the branches and find plentiful food in the shallow water rich in marine life.

THE MANGROVES AT NABQ

The Nabq zone became a protected area and an extension of the Ras Mohammed National Park in 1992. It covers a total surface of 600 square kilometers at the end of the Wadi Kid and boasts the largest mangrove (Avicenia marina) forest in Sinai. The mangroves at Nabq run for four kilometers along the coast—from the small village of el-Ghargana, inhabited by Bedouin fishermen, to the Ras Atantur promontory—occupying the sandy zone between the strand and the outer slopes of the coral reef. The Nabq reserve has a Visitors Center that provides tourists with all necessary information concerning the biological aspects of the territory. The extremely complex mangrove ecosystem is the habitat of 134 species of terrestrial plants and 7 species of algae.

A fiddler crab (Uca sp.)

Detail of Avicenia marina's *flowers and leaves dotted with white salt crystals*

The Visitor Center in Nabq

The Desert

*T*he desert landscape is the predominating element of Sinai, covering almost the entire surface of the peninsula. It is extremely varied in both color and form, an exceptional mineral universe in which nature has created splendid, singular sculptures out of the rock.

A typical erosion shape called a 'mushroom'

Sand resulting from disintegrated granite

The Sinai desert is very arid due to the meager rainfall and the rapid evaporation caused by the high daytime temperature. It is a complex ecosystem with different types of plants that have adapted to this difficult, hostile environment and an interesting, heterogeneous fauna that includes wild goats, foxes, rodents, gazelles, reptiles, raptors, and numerous insectivores. The Sinai desert is for the most part mountainous and rocky, with limited stretches of sandy areas mostly located in the central Tih Plateau that were created by the pulverization of the rocks by meteors. The presence of a craggy mountain range whose peaks are often over 2,000 meters high attenuates the aridity of the desert to some degree and favors the growth of vegetation. The mass of crystalline rocks, sandstone, and limestone in the Sinai

A very narrow wadi carved in sandstone

Wadis are the fossil beds of age-old rivers

peninsula is cut through by a maze of valleys, the *wadis*, which are often parallel and can be dozens of kilometers long and hundreds of meters wide, or may be so weakly developed that they may be merely crevices in the rock. The wadis are the fossil beds of age-old rivers that ran through the region in the Quaternary Era, when there was much more rainfall, and that deeply eroded the rock beds. Often the wadis begin at the foot of a rock face where there is a spring surrounded by shrubs and, occasionally, groups of palm trees; after finishing their course they flow into larger wadis or fan out into the coastal zone.

A wadi with its stream

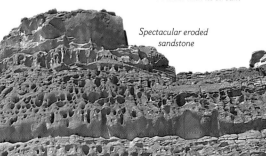

Spectacular eroded sandstone

The Oases

*O*ases are special areas in the desert that because of their geomorphological conformation have water and are fertile; this attracts the Bedouin, who settle around them.

Irrigation canal

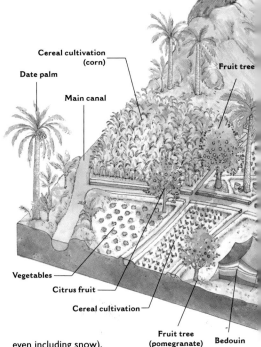

Cereal cultivation (corn)

Date palm

Main canal

Fruit tree

Vegetables

Citrus fruit

Cereal cultivation

Fruit tree (pomegranate)

Bedouin tent

In the Sinai desert the presence of underground water and springs is not as rare as one might imagine when first seeing this mineral universe consisting of impressive, massive, sun-baked rock and impassable peaks. Indeed, the rough terrain and its geographic position between the Mediterranean and the Red Sea favor rare precipitation (sometimes even including snow), particularly from late autumn to spring. The average annual rainfall in

A well in the Ain Khudra oasis

the mountainous central-southern region is 250–300 millimeters. However, even this slight rainfall is enough to form springs, provided the rainwater, during its underground course, runs over strata of almost impermeable rock such as marly limestone or clay, which prevent it from being dispersed in

these verdant areas, digging wells that allowed them to create canal networks to irrigate the surrounding area and make it suitable for growing cereals (wheat, corn), vegetables such as tomatoes and lettuce, and

Dates

fruit (apples, oranges, lemons, pomegranates, and mangos). Thus a rudimentary form of agriculture has developed in the oases that, together with livestock raising (dromedaries—commonly called camels—goats, sheep, chickens, and pigeons), guarantees a means of subsistence to the Bedouin community.

Dromedary

Mango tree

Secondary canals

Sheep

the subsurface and sometimes causes the water table to rise to the surface of the ground. The increase in humidity in the terrain makes for luxuriant vegetation, from palm trees to wild shrubs and grasses. This creates oases, around which there are human settlements.

Since very ancient times the desert dwellers learned to exploit to the full the water supplies in

THE LARGEST OASIS IN SINAI

The Feiran Oasis, which stretches for more than 5 km in the Wadi Feiran, the most important and largest valley in the peninsula, is the largest oasis in Sinai, situated on the slopes of the Meharret and Tahuna mountains. Over 30,000 palm trees provide a great amount of dates to the inhabitants, who practice intensive cultivation in the oasis irrigated by a small watercourse fed by numerous wells, backwater tanks, and a network of small canals.

HISTORY, COSTUMS, TRADITIONS

Prehistoric Sinai

Sinai and the Pharaohs

Nabataeans-Ottomans

Contemporary History

The Bedouin in Sinai

Prehistoric Sinai

Prehistoric graffitos

Despite its harsh climate and lack of water, there are many traces of settlements in Sinai dating back to the pre-ceramics phase of the Neolithic period (7000–5000 B.C.).

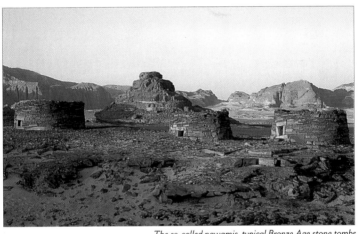

The so-called nawamis, typical Bronze Age stone tombs

As early as the Upper Paleolithic and pre-ceramics Neolithic periods the turquoise and copper deposits in Sinai attracted populations from the east as well as from the north. These mining colonists migrated slowly southward, stopping at the areas richest in minerals. In the Timna culture period (around 3500 B.C.) copper mining and smelting developed to a considerable degree, triggering an increase in the Sinai populations, which, in the Serabit el-Khadem region, also mined turquoise.

The early Bronze Age (end of the fourth millennium B.C.) witnessed the use of numerous stone tombs known as *nawamis* (which in Arabic means "mosquitoes") that are attributed to the seminomadic populations who probably arrived from northern Egypt and were engaged in mining activity.

Local copper

A nawamis

Sinai and the Pharaohs

The goddess Hathor

*T*he deposits of turqoise and copper—the latter indispensable for the development of ancient technology—attracted the attention of the ancient Egyptian rulers as early as the beginning of the third millennium B.C.

The temple at Serabit el-Khadem

As early as the Thinite period (Naqada II culture, around the mid-fourth millennium B.C.) the Egyptians invaded the northernmost areas of Sinai, subduing the Timna populations, and from the 3rd Dynasty on (2670–2570 B.C.) they began to send expeditions to systematically exploit the copper and turquoise deposits there. However, the pharaohs never really colonized Sinai, as their intervention consisted only of sending mining expeditions and setting up work camps near the mines. Their mining activity reached its height in the 12th Dynasty (1955–1750 B.C.), during the rule of Amenemhet III: a huge slag heap, weighing about 100,000 tons and dating from this period, was found at Bir Nasib. Serabit el-Khadem has the most important copper and turquoise mines on a

Sinai turquoise

THE FIRST ALPHABET

Few people know that on the walls of a mine a short distance from the temple of Serabit, archaeologists found inscriptions that probably date back to the Middle Kingdom and are one of the earliest examples of Semitic alphabetic script in history. It has been partly deciphered and is called 'protosinaitic script.'

THE EXODUS AND MOUNT SINAI

Mediterranean Sea

Pithom · Lake Timsah · **B**

Kadesh Barnea

S I N A I

E G Y P T

Gulf of Suez

Ezion-Gaber

Gebel Musa · **A**

Gulf of Aqaba

A *Southern route*   **B** *Northern route*

According to tradition the Israelites left the eastern Delta region (from Piramesse or Pithom) during Ramesses II's rule and went to Sinai by crossing the Red Sea (Exodus 14) at an unspecified locality that may be identified as Lake Timsah or the southern tip of Lake Manzala. They then proceeded southward to the 'Mountain of God,' or present-day Mount Sinai, and then went to Ezion-Gaber and again went northward in the direction of Kadesh Barnea, which became the main base of the Israelites for the conquest of their promised land.

However, this hypothetical route of the Exodus is quite improbable: not only is it illogical, but it would also have been extremely difficult and unfeasible, given the scarcity of water necessary for an expedition on the part of so many people. Recently, scholars opted for the 'northern route,' which is more realistic because the first leg is parallel to the Mediterranean coast and then the route heads southward to Mt. Har Harkhom, now in Israel: this is most probably the geographic site where the biblical 'Mount Sinai' was located.

plateau 850 meters a.s.l. that covers an area of 20 square kilometers and ends in a rocky rampart. Here the miners built a walled sacred precinct with a temple during the rule of Sesostris I (12th Dynasty). Further building activity was carried out under Amenemhet II, III, and IV: the pharaohs' chapel, the rock-hewn chapel dedicated to the goddess Hathor, the 'Mistress of Turquoise,' under whose protection the mines were placed in the Middle Kingdom, and the adjacent rock chapel initially dedicated to the

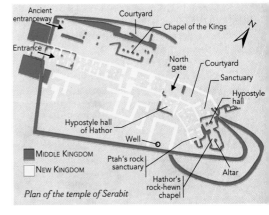

Ancient entranceway · Courtyard · Chapel of the Kings

Entrance · North gate · Courtyard · Sanctuary · Hypostyle hall

Hypostyle hall of Hathor · Well

MIDDLE KINGDOM · NEW KINGDOM · Ptah's rock sanctuary · Altar · Hathor's rock-hewn chapel

Plan of the temple of Serabit

Memphite god Ptah (both these chapels had a portico). However, the temple at Serabit that we see today dates from the

New Kingdom, when a series of halls were added that extended the original structure toward the southwest.

From the Nabataeans to the Ottomans

Nabataean graffito

The mihrab in the mosque at the Qalat el-Gundi fortress

*F*or centuries, the ancient Romans, Nabataean traders, Christian monks and hermits, Mamluks, and Ottoman Turks used Sinai as a communication route.

A major route to Syria and the East in the Roman period (2nd century A.D.), Sinai was crossed by the caravans of the Nabataean traders who, from the 2nd to the 4th century A.D., left many graffiti on the faces of the wadis to attest to their passage there. From the 4th century on, Sinai was colonized by the early Christians (cenobitic and anchoritic monks),

becoming an increasingly popular pilgrimage site as well. The Arabs conquered Egypt in 640 but at first showed no interest in Sinai, which was used only as a route for Muslim pilgrims, who passed through Eilat and Aqaba on their way to Mecca. Only centuries later, in 1182, did Salah el-Din (known as 'Saladin' in the Western world) conquer *Graye Island* (present-day

Pharaoh's Island) near Nuweiba, which was controlled by the Crusaders, and enlarge the massive fortress already there; in 1187 he built another one, Qalat el-Gundi, near Ras Sidr. In the early 16th century the Mamluk sultan El-Ghuri had two more fortresses built at Nakhl and Nuweiba. Lastly, the Ottoman Turks, who conquered Egypt in 1517, fortified the cities of El-Tor and El-Arish.

The fortress on Pharaoh's Island

The Scientific Exploration of Sinai

In the early 18th century the geography, topography, fauna, and flora of Sinai were virtually unknown. Scientific study of the region was begun by the Swedish naturalist Peter Forskal in 1761 and was continued by the German Eduard Rüppel in 1818–28.

Linant de Bellefonds and Léon de Laborde studying the temple at Serabit el-Khadem in 1828

In 1761, on board the ship *Arabia Felix* bound for Yemen, was the Swedish botanist Peter Förskal, a member of the scientific expedition organized by the German Carsten Niebuhr, who could be considered the first explorer of Sinai and the Red Sea. Förskal began the scientific study

An original drawing by Rüppel

of the Red Sea, examining and identifying for the first time 58 species of fish. His studies were continued in 1818 by the German naturalist Eduard Rüppel, who discovered 175 other species of fish and initiated the study of the terrestrial fauna of the region. Rüppel is also to be credited for having made the first topographical

Eduard Rüppel

survey of Sinai and having drawn up the first reliable map of the peninsula. In 1820 the Sienese physician and draftsman Alessandro Ricci made the first drawing of the temple at Serabit el-Khadem. He was followed in 1828 by the French architect Linant de Bellefonds together with his friend Léon de Laborde; they explored central Sinai and also made drawings and relief maps of Serabit.

Contemporary History

*A*n extremely important territory from a strategic standpoint because of its position between Egypt and Israel and its western border being the Suez Canal, Sinai was the theater of three wars between 1956 and 1973. Peace was restored to the region only in 1978 thanks to the Camp David agreement.

President Nasser had two cannons placed at Ras Nasrani, opposite Tiran Island, thus ensuring Egypt total control of the Strait of Tiran. This act triggered the first Israeli–Egyptian war.

On 26 October 1956, after the Suez Canal had been nationalized by Colonel Gamal Abdel Nasser, the president of the new Arab Republic of Egypt, the Israelis launched an attack in Sinai. On November 5 General Moshe Dayan entered Sharm el-Sheikh with his troops, but they returned to Israel thanks to the intervention of the United Nations. In 1967, when Nasser set up a blockade of the Strait of Tiran, Israel decided to make a preventive attack against Egypt and so the 'Six-Day War' began on June 5, after

An Israeli tank

1967

An MPO ship patrolling the Strait of Tiran

which Sinai passed under Israeli control. In 1978 the President of Egypt, Anwar Sadat, and Israeli Prime Minister Menahem Begin signed the Camp David agreement, which put an end to a long period of hostility between the two nations. The Israeli troops left Sinai, which was then divided into three sectors that were to be demilitarized gradually: zone A (**A**lfa), zone B (**B**ravo) and zone C (**C**harlie).

An MFO soldier

THE CREATION OF THE MFO

In 1982 an independent multinational force was created to guarantee the 'buffer zone' status of Sinai, to verify that the Israelis and Egyptians were respecting the Camp David agreement, and to ensure the free transit of ships in the Strait of Tiran. The force was called MFO (Multinational Force & Observers) and was financed by Israel, Egypt, and the United States. The components of the MFO are of different nationalities (Americans, Australians, Canadians, Colombians, Fijians, Frenchmen, Italians,

New Zealanders, and Uruguayans) and are based in two camps in zone C, where Egypt has the right to keep only police forces: the North Camp near El-Arish and South Camp at Sharm el-Sheikh.

The dove of peace, the MFO symbol

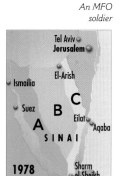

1978

The Bedouin in Sinai

*T*he Bedouin are the original inhabitants of the deserts and mountains in Sinai, who once lived exclusively on small animals and agriculture.

A young Bedouin belonging to the Muzeina tribe

Bedouin jewelry

A Bedouin tent

*T*hese people came from places around the Sinai peninsula such as Palestine, Jordan, and Arabia and settled in this difficult environment. Until a few years ago they managed to preserve their traditional way of life and customs. The Bedouin can be divided into different tribes, homogeneous social groups that take in individuals with the same origin and traditions. They lived on livestock breeding and, sometimes, rudimentary forms of agriculture. Living in such a harsh and barren environment as the desert, this population has always had to live a nomadic life, moving around in rather extended but well-defined areas. Consequently, tents, which are easy to carry on a camel, became their typical dwelling place as well as the center of their social life. They are made of heavy camel's-hair cloth usually dyed in dark colors (the Bedouin

A Bedouin woman with her face covered with the classic burqu'

A grindstone for grain

in the Near and Middle East are also known as "the black tent people") and held up by a complicated system of wooden palm tree poles set into the ground. Tents shelter the Bedouin from the torrid summer heat and the biting cold of winter nights. Generally, the tents of a tribe are placed next to one another in the camps situated at the foot of a mountain near wells (*bir* in Arabic), springs (*ain*) or small oases (*waha*). This traditional lifestyle is now in rapid decline for many reasons, the most important of which is the rise of tourism, which has become the main source of income for many of the 80,000 or so Bedouin in Sinai, especially those (about 25,000) who live in the region between St. Catherine's, Sharm el-

CAMELS

The word "camel" derives from the Arabic gamal. *Camels* (Camelus dromedarius) *are the animals best adapted to the desert climate because they consume very little water and can go for more than ten*

began to be used from the 7th century B.C. on. The Bedouin use camels not only as a means of transport and for farmwork, but also as food; their meat has the same consistency as beef. Camel's hair is used for fabrics, rugs, and other handicraft products.

Camel saddle

days without drinking. The camel was domesticated in Arabia in the third millennium B.C. but was unknown in ancient Egypt until it

A Bedouin of the Tarabin tribe at Nuweiba

Sheikh, Dahab, and Nuweiba. Now that many of them have jobs in the tourist industry, the Bedouin have gradually abandoned their former nomadic way of life and have become sedentary: their tents are being replaced by corrugated iron sheds and stone houses, and their camels have given way to trucks.

THE SITES

Ras Mohammed

Sharm el-Sheikh

Dahab

Nuweiba

The Region of St. Catherine's

El-Tor

A house built of blocks of fossil coral

*T*his town was the main port in the northern Red Sea until the Suez Canal was opened. Now El-Tor is the capital of the governorate of South Sinai.

The present-day port at El-Tor

El-Tor is a city on the southwestern coast of Sinai 230 kilometers from the Ahmed Hamdi Tunnel under the Suez Canal that allows travelers to reach Sinai by land. The name of the city seems to have derived from the Greek *To Oros* (the mountain), referring to the mountain east of El-Tor, which was always a major commercial port thanks to its position on the Gulf of Suez. Here the ships unloaded merchandise from Arabia and Africa, which was put in the many warehouses made of blocks of local fossil coral.

The Ottomans, rulers of Egypt from 1517, built a fortress at El-Tor that in 1858 was converted into a lazaretto to quarantine pilgrims coming from Mecca. The city was also an important Christian monastic center from the 4th century on and in the hinterland a monastery (later destroyed) was built at the same time as St. Catherine's. In the 16th century another monastery was founded near the port; it was completely rebuilt by the monks from St. Catherine's in 1875 and dedicated to St. George.

The El-Tor monastery

Ras Mohammed National Park

The Ras Mohammed peninsula seen from the south

*R*as Mohammed, declared a national park in 1983 by the Egyptian government, is the most famous nature site in Sinai and has become one of the greatest tourist attractions in Egypt.

NATIONAL PARKS OF EGYPT

*A*bout twenty kilometers south of Sharm el-Sheikh (eight miles by sea) is the wild peninsula of *Ras Mohammed* ('Muhammad's Cape'), the southernmost part of Sinai and one of the loveliest and most interesting sites in the Red Sea.

This is an unspoiled area of extraordinary beauty and natural importance and therefore

A triggerfish

became a national park in 1983. It consists of a slightly elevated promontory made up of fossil coral reefs that emerged after a change in the coastline that occurred some 70,000 years ago. The park is bordered by magnificent coral reefs that are particularly well developed in the southern part, which is the habitat of a great many

species of fish, including many that normally live in the open sea. The spectacular coral formations and the unique abundance of fauna have made Ras Mohammed famous throughout the world. Being the southernmost tip of Sinai,

A park ranger

A batfish

Ras Mohammed is the meeting point of two very different water masses: the Gulf of Aqaba, to the east, has

A coral grouper

deep and clear water with less salinity than the Gulf of Suez, which is very salty and not very deep. The concentration of flora and fauna that results from this is almost unrivalled any-where in the world: over 1,000 species of tropical fish, 170 species of corals, and an infinite number of sponges and gorgonians.

Different ecosystems co-exist at Ras Mohammed, interacting in a very complex manner: the coral reef, mangroves, and dunes. Because of its excep-tional beauty and enor-mous scientific and natural significance, the

Ras Mohammed

Egyptian government decided to protect the entire area from any possible harm arising from the indiscriminate growth of tourism in the region that could alter its ecology for ever. Law no.

A blue-spotted stingray

and as such is subject to a series of regulations that safeguard it.

A school of jackfish

A Napoleon fish

102, passed in 1983, states that the Ras Mohammed area, inclu-ding the islands and coral formations in the Strait of Tiran, is a national park

The *Ras Mohammed Marine Protected Area* covers an area of 97 square kilometers along the Gulf of Aqaba, equal to 0.6% of the entire Egyptian coast. Here construction of tourist facilities or industrial buildings is strictly forbidden, as are fishing and hunting, camping outside the designated campgrounds (where visitors have to ask the Park Management for permission to camp). Furthermore, tourists must respect the park regulations; failure to do so will result in disci-plinary measures, which may range from being expelled from the park to being brought before the Egyptian courts of law.

Sharm el-Sheikh and Naama Bay

Aerial view of Sharm el-Sheikh

S*harm el-Sheikh, the tourist capital of Sinai, together with neighboring Naama Bay, has grown tremendously in a short time, becoming the most famous seaside resort in the Red Sea.*

The beach at Naama Bay

The town of Sharm el-Sheikh (the Arabic word *sharm* means 'bay' and the toponym may be translated as 'the Sheikh's Bay') was founded in 1967–1970, during the Israeli occupation, over a high rocky spur formed by a fossil coral reef that dominates the large bay of *Sharm el-Maya*. Next to this is another bay, *Sharm el-Sheikh*, which now has a busy tourist, commercial, and military port. Many tourist and hotel facilities have risen up around the beach bordering Sharm el-Maya and, a bit further north, around a marvelous bay that is the outlet to the sea of a broad wadi the Bedouin call *Marsa el-Aat*, now known as Naama Bay.

Today Sharm el-Sheikh and Naama Bay, which is only a few kilometers from the Ras Nasrani International Airport, have become the leading tourist resorts not only of Sinai, but of the entire Red Sea, as well as extremely popular diving centers.

Water sports in Naama Bay

Dahab

Because of its geographic position, Dahab is almost constantly exposed to the wind and has consequently become a favorite with windsurfers.

The famous dune of Dahab

Aerial view of the Bay of Qura and Dahab

The coral peninsula of Dahab—an Arabic word that means 'gold,' a clear allusion to the yellow rocks and sand on its splendid beaches—is situated between *Qura Bay* to the south and small *Ghazala Bay* to the north, which boasts the most picturesque Bedouin village in Sinai, *Asala*, that is surrounded by tall palm trees and is known for its handicrafts. This locality attracts the many Bedouin in the area as well as ever growing numbers of tourists (usually young ones) in search of adventure in an informal and exotic setting.

The mountains immediately north of Dahab make for pleasant excursions in off-road vehicles, for example at *Wadi Qnai* and 'Wadi Connection.'

At Dahab the great size of the coral formations makes it ideal for diving. All the dive sites can be reached by land, but you can also rent a boat to get to them. Among the most interesting, mention should be made of the famous *Canyon* and *Blue Hole*, which, however, should be used only by expert divers.

The Bedouin village of Asala

Nuweiba

*T*his locality is known as the 'pearl of the Gulf of Aqaba' because of its beautiful coast bordered by tall palm trees, but it recently became famous thanks to a dolphin.

A Bedouin fisherwoman

The beach at Nuweiba

*N*uweiba is not only a rapidly growing seaside resort, but also has a large commercial port with regular ship and hydrofoil service to Aqaba, in Jordan, which can be reached in 90 minutes, so that it has become an ideal starting point for those who want to visit Petra, the legendary capital of the Natabaean kingdom. Nuweiba consists of a southern sector called *Nuweiba Muzeina* because it is inhabited by Bedouin of the Muzeina tribe, and a northern sector known as *Nuweiba el-Tarabin*, where the Bedouin of the Tarabin tribe live. Here there is a massive fortress built by the sultan El-Ghuri in the 16th century, at the end of the important track that connected the Gulf of Aqaba, St. Catherine's Monastery, and the Gulf

The coast at Ras Abu Galum, south of Nuweiba

Sultan El-Ghuri's fortress

of Suez, to protect the caravan routes to Mecca and Jerusalem.

In recent years more and more tourists have gone to Nuweiba to see

The dolphin at Nuweiba

another attraction. A charming and sociable female dolphin has decided to settle in a bay in the southern part of town at the end of the coastal track that links Nuweiba and Ras Abu Galum and has been 'adopted' by the local Bedouin, so visitors can swim with a dolphin and observe it at close range in its natural habitat.

Monument to the dolphin in Nuweiba

The protected area of Ras Abu Galum, like the one at Nabq, was made part of the Ras Mohammed National Park in keeping with the Environment Ministry's policy of safeguarding the land. The Ras Abu Galum zone lies far away from the traditional visitors' route and is known for its wild beauty. Despite this, only recently was it considered a major factor in the natural balance of the environment and of the Bedouin populations that inhabit the area, whose economy is based almost exclusively on fishing.

COLORED CANYON

Not far from the small Ain Furtaga oasis about 12 kilometers north of Nuweiba, going up the Wadi Watir, one of the most beautiful valleys in the Sinai peninsula that connects the town and the El-Naqb international airport, is the beginning of the track that goes to

one of the geological wonders of Sinai—the Colored Canyon. The narrow sandstone sides of the canyon, which in some sections are 40 meters high and only one meter apart, contain ferrous oxide and manganese, which produce an incredible gamut of colors, from dark brown to red and straw yellow.

Taba

This town a few hundred meters from the Egyptian–Israeli border is the center of a region rich in natural attractions.

A modern rock carving in the Wadi Umm Sideira, in the interior of Taba

The Taba promontory

Taba lies near the frontier of Israel, which delimits the Egyptian coast of the Red Sea to the north.

Centuries ago the town was an important transit point for the caravans that traveled along the Aqaba track and stopped there to draw water from the local well. The name Taba is documented only from 1906, when the British

THE FJORD

The so-called fjord, the most beautiful and striking inlet in the entire Gulf of Aqaba, is 12 kilometers south of Taba and 53 km from Nuweiba. The shallow water is a splendid blue-turquoise, and the road descends right to the sandy beach and then goes up the northern side of the bay to a scenic viewpoint. By continuing northward for six kilometers one arrives at Pharaoh's Island.

marked out the eastern frontier between Egypt and the Ottoman Empire by following a line that went from Rafah on the Mediterranean coast to Taba at the Red Sea. Sinai was given back to Egypt in stages between 1978 and 1982, but the Israelis kept control of Taba until 1989, when the present-day frontier was established.

One of the main features in the town is the Hilton Taba Hotel and its facilities, built by the Israelis and then sold to Egypt. In recent times Taba has become a very important tourist center thanks to the construction of the nearby El-Naqb international airport and other hotels.

Since 1988 Taba and the surroundings have been made part of the protected areas of Sinai in order to safeguard their scenic beauty, including the *Colored Valley*, formed by an age-old river that cut through the multicolored sandstone; the valley floor now has a wide and panoramic asphalt road that leads to El-Arish, a seaside resort along the Mediterranean Sea. On the sides of one of the lateral wadis of the Colored Valley there are important inscriptions dating from the Nabataean and Roman periods.

PHARAOH'S ISLAND

A few miles after the Fjord is the extremely beautiful Pharaoh's Island (Geziret el-Faraun in Arabic), a site that is interesting from both a natural and a historic standpoint. This island, identified with the famous Phoenician port known as Ezion-Gaber, has a fortress that was built during the Byzantine period, occupied by the Crusaders in 1116, and conquered in 1182 by the sultan Saladin, who enlarged it. The fortress was restored and opened to the public in 1986. On the northeastern coast of the island (formerly called Coral Island), where the coral reefs are more developed, there is a site that is particularly suitable for dives to the bottom, which is 10–15 meters deep.

The Colored Valley

The Region of St. Catherine's

*T*he famous St. Catherine's Monastery was built by the emperor Justinian at the foot of the holy mountain (Mount Sinai) where Moses received the Tables of the Law. Since the Middle Ages it has been a major Christian pilgrimage site.

Aerial view of St. Catherine's Monastery

*T*he region of St. Catherine's has an area of 4,300 square kilometers and is the largest protected area in the Sinai peninsula. The climate and nature combine to create a unique landscape with interesting flora and fauna (there are gazelles, foxes, stone martens, ibexes, many species of birds, raptors, and reptiles) that have adapted amazingly well to the difficult environmental conditions.

The region is known for its monastery, which lies 1,570 meters a.s.l. at the foot of Mount Sinai, 'Moses' Mountain,' at whose peak the prophet

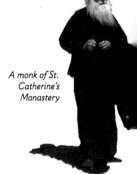

A monk of St. Catherine's Monastery

received the Ten Commandments. The monastery was built during the reign of the emperor Justinian (6th century) on the site where, according to tradition, Moses saw the burning bush (*Exodus, 3, 2*). The impressive wall surrounding it is partly made up of the buildings

St. Catherine's monastery

A 12th-century icon

and dates back to the same period. Only in the 11th century was the monastery dedicated to St. Catherine, a young Christian martyr from Alexandria who died in the late 4th century. According to the legend, her body was miraculously found on the top of a mountain near Mount Sinai, which was then called *Gebel Katrin*, or Mt. Catherine. The mountain, 2,637 meters high, is the highest in the Sinai peninsula and in Egypt. Today only a small section of the monastery is open to the public: the Byzantine-style two-aisle basilica; 'Moses' well,' traditionally considered the spot where the prophet met his future wife Zipporah (*Exodus 2, 21*); the 'burning bush';

Wall decoration

MOSES' MOUNTAIN

One of the classic tours in the St. Catherine's Monastery zone consists of the walk up Gebel Musa, literally 'Moses' Mountain,' Mount Sinai in the Bible, where Moses was traditionally thought to have received the Ten Commandments. The peak of Mount Sinai, where there is a chapel built in 1934 over the remains of a 5th-century church, can be reached via two trails that both start at the monastery. The first, called Sikket el-Basha (the Pasha's path), is the one usually used for the climb; it follows a stretch of the monastery valley (Wadi el-Deir). The other one, called Sikket Sayyidna Musa (path of our Lord Moses), was the ancient path used by the monks; it is more direct but fatiguing as it consists of 3,700 steps carved out of the rock. The climb takes two or three hours, but from the top of the mountain there is an incomparable view of all of south Sinai.

The chapel on Mount Sinai

the monks' garden, and the ossuary. Visitors are not allowed in the library (which some scholars say is the second most important after the Vatican Library), the old refectory, or the Chapel of the Burning Bush. Today St. Catherine's monastery is the home of about fifteen Eastern Orthodox monks under the guidance of the Archbishop of St. Catherine's.

El-Arish and North Sinai

*E*l-Arish is the largest town in the Sinai peninsula and the administrative capial of the North Sinai governorate. It is famous for an extensive beach washed by the Mediterranean and bordered by a huge palm grove.

The palm grove at El-Arish along the beach on the Mediterranean Sea

The city of El-Arish lies on the Mediterranean coast of Sinai, is the capital of North Sinai, and has a population of over 70,000. It owes its fame as a seaside resort to its huge, sandy beach that is bordered by a great expanse of palm trees that extends for several kilometers. The Egyptian outpost during the Ptolemaic and Roman periods, the city was fortified during the Middle Ages and then during the Ottoman period; only a few traces of these constructions have been preserved in the quarter where the large Bedouin market is held every Thursday, when all the nomads in the region gather together. In fact, El-Arish is considered the most important town in Sinai for Bedouin handicrafts and also boasts the *Sinai Heritage Museum*, the only museum

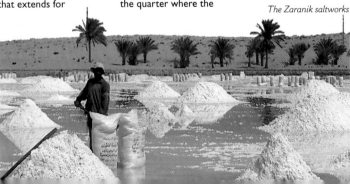

The Zaranik saltworks

The lagoons at Zaranik

in the peninsula given over to Bedouin culture. About thirty kilometers west of El-Arish is the *Protected Area of Zaranik* which, together with the nearby *Bardawil Lagoon*, is

محميـــة الزرانيـــق
شمــال سينــاء - مصر

The symbol of Zaranik

an important transit point for migratory birds. Indeed, 270 species of birds have been identified at Zaranik, and about a dozen nest in this area.

Sunset at El-Arish

PELUSIUM

West of Zaranik are the impressive ruins of ancient city of Pelusium, now known as Tell el-Farama or simply Farma. The ruins extend over a vast area that was excavated and studied in a systematic manner only recently. Pelusium, which derives from the Greek Pelusion and means 'marsh,' lay on the Pelusium arm of the Nile. It was an important city as long ago as the pharaonic age and controlled the major caravan route that connected Egypt with Palestine and Syria. Tradition has it that the Holy Family stopped at Pelusium during the flight to Egypt. The city became an important port and trade and cultural center under the Romans and remained so during the Early Christian period, becoming a bishopric in the 4th century. The silting up of the Pelusium branch of the Nile brought about the gradual decline of the city from the 7th century on.

ESSENTIAL BIBLIOGRAPHY

Bemert, G., R. Ormond. *Red Sea Coral Reefs*. Boston, London, 1981.
Goodman, S. M., P. L. Meininger. *The Birds of Egypt*. Oxford, 1989.
Jahn, W. and R. *Sinai and the Red Sea*. Cairo, 1997
Palmer, E. H. *The Desert of Exodus: Journey on Foot in the Wilderness of the Forty Years Wandering*. Cambridge, 1871.
Petrie, F. *Researches in Sinai*. London, 1906.
Randall, J. E. *Red Sea Fishes*. London, 1986.
Rothenberg, B., H. Weyer. *Sinai*. Berne, 1979.
Schmidt, N. *Sinai und Rotes Meer: Reise-Handbook*. Cologne, 1988.
Siliotti, A. *Guida all'Esplorazione del Sinai*. Vercelli, 1994.
Siliotti, A. *Sharm el-Sheikh Diving Guide*. Cairo, 1999.
Valbelle, D., C. Bonnet. *Le sanctuaire d'Hathor maîtresse de la turquoise*. Paris, 1996
Vine, P. *Red Sea Invertebrates*. London, 1986.

PHOTOGRAPH CREDITS

All the photographs in this book are by Alberto Siliotti/Archivio Image Service - Geodia except for the following:
Claudio Concina: pages 22 below, 34 fourth from the top, 39 below, 41 right above and below;
Manfred Bortoli: diving photos on pages 14, 15, 16,17, 36, 37 41.

DRAWINGS

All the drawings in this book are by Stefania Cossu except for the following:
Simone Boni 2nd and 3rd page of cover.